# TOP HIGH SCHOOL SPORTS
# CHEERLEADING

# LOS MEJORES DEPORTES DE LA ESCUELA SECUNDARIA
# PORRISMO

A Crabtree Branches Book
Un libro de Las Ramas de Crabtree

WRITTEN BY / ESCRITO POR THOMAS KINGSLEY TROUPE
TRANSLATED BY / TRADUCCIÓN DE SANTIAGO OCHOA

Crabtree Publishing
crabtreebooks.com

# School-to-Home Support for Caregivers and Teachers

This high-interest book is designed to motivate striving students with engaging topics while building fluency, vocabulary, and an interest in reading. Here are a few questions and activities to help the reader build upon his or her comprehension skills.

## Before Reading:

- *What do I think this book is about?*
- *What do I know about this topic?*
- *What do I want to learn about this topic?*
- *Why am I reading this book?*

## During Reading:

- *I wonder why...*
- *I'm curious to know...*
- *How is this like something I already know?*
- *What have I learned so far?*

## After Reading:

- *What was the author trying to teach me?*
- *What are some details?*
- *How did the photographs and captions help me understand more?*
- *Read the book again and look for the vocabulary words.*
- *What questions do I still have?*

## Extension Activities:

- *What was your favorite part of the book? Write a paragraph on it.*
- *Draw a picture of your favorite thing you learned from the book.*

# Apoyos de la escuela a los hogares para cuidadores y maestros

Este libro de alto interés está diseñado para motivar a los estudiantes dedicados con temas atractivos, mientras desarrollan la fluidez, el vocabulario y el interés por la lectura. A continuación se presentan algunas preguntas y actividades para ayudar al lector a desarrollar sus habilidades de comprensión.

## Antes de leer:

- *¿De qué pienso que trata este libro?*
- *¿Qué sé sobre este tema?*
- *¿Qué quiero aprender sobre este tema?*
- *¿Por qué estoy leyendo este libro?*

## Durante la lectura:

- *Me pregunto por qué...*
- *Tengo curiosidad de saber...*
- *¿En qué se parece esto a algo que ya conozco?*
- *¿Qué he aprendido hasta ahora?*

## Después de la lectura:

- *¿Qué intentaba enseñarme el autor?*
- *¿Cuáles son algunos detalles?*
- *¿Cómo me ayudaron las fotografías y los pies de foto a entender más?*
- *Vuelve a leer el libro y busca las palabras del vocabulario.*
- *¿Qué preguntas tengo aún?*

## Actividades de extensión:

- *¿Cuál fue tu parte favorita del libro? Escribe un párrafo sobre ella.*
- *Haz un dibujo de lo que más te gustó del libro.*

# TABLE OF CONTENTS



# ÍNDICE

# GIVE ME A V!
# ¡DAME UNA V!

The crowd groans as the home team loses a big play on the field. You and your cheerleading squad know what to do. The music blares as you and your teammates dance and get the fans in the stands chanting. In no time, the crowd is on their feet, cheering their team to victory!

El público grita cuando el equipo local pierde una gran jugada en el campo. Tú y tu equipo de animadoras saben qué hacer. La música suena mientras tú y tus compañeras de equipo bailan y hacen corear a los aficionados en las gradas. ¡En poco tiempo, el público se pone de pie y anima a su equipo a la victoria!

Grab your pom-poms and megaphone! We're about to learn why cheerleading ranks among the...TOP HIGH SCHOOL SPORTS.

Agarra los pompones y el megáfono. Estamos a punto de saber por qué el porrismo se encuentra entre los... MEJORES DEPORTES DE LA ESCUELA SECUNDARIA.

**FUN FACT** **DATO CURIOSO**

Cheerleading is considered one of the most dangerous sports for girls. Injuries include broken bones, concussions, and torn ligaments, like the **ACL**.

El porrismo está considerado como uno de los deportes más peligrosos para las chicas. Las lesiones incluyen huesos rotos, contusiones cerebrales y rotura de ligamentos, como el **LCA**.

# CHEERLEADING HISTORY
# HISTORIA DEL PORRISMO

Cheerleading started in Great Britain during in the 1860s. In the 1880s, cheerleading reached the United States. Thomas Peebles introduced the idea of chanting to **spectators** at the University of Minnesota. There, Johnny Campbell led the first organized cheer during a game against Princeton University in 1898.

El porrismo comenzó en Gran Bretaña en la década de 1860. Llegó a Estados Unidos en la década de 1880. Thomas Peebles introdujo la idea de cantar a los espectadores en la Universidad de Minnesota. Allí, Johnny Campbell dirigió la primera animación organizada durante un partido contra la Universidad de Princeton en 1898.

At the time, cheerleading was a male-dominated sport. It wasn't until the 1920s that women became involved in cheerleading.

En aquella época, el porrismo era un deporte dominado por los hombres. No fue hasta la década de 1920 que las mujeres se involucraron en el porrismo.

## A CHEER FROM PRINCETON (1884) / UNA PORRA PARA PRINCETON (1884):

*Ray, Ray, Ray!*
*Tiger, Tiger, Tiger!*
*Sis, Sis, Sis!*
*Boom, Boom, Boom*
*Aaaaah! Princeton,*
*Princeton, Princeton!*

**Four United States Presidents were cheerleaders years before their big job at the White House. They included Franklin D. Roosevelt from Harvard College, Dwight D. Eisenhower at West Point, Ronald Reagan for Eureka College, and George W. Bush while he attended Phillips Academy. Hooray for America!**

**Cuatro presidentes de Estados Unidos fueron porristas años antes de su importante trabajo en la Casa Blanca. Entre ellos, Franklin D. Roosevelt en el Harvard College, Dwight D. Eisenhower en West Point, Ronald Reagan en el Eureka College y George W. Bush mientras asistía a la Academia Phillips. ¡Hurra por Estados Unidos!**

# WHY CHEERLEADING?
# ¿POR QUÉ EL PORRISMO?

Cheerleading is an important part of high school sports. Cheerleaders not only encourage school spirit, but use their **enthusiasm** and energy to bring the team and the crowd together.

El porrismo es una parte importante de los deportes de la escuela secundaria. El porrismo no solo fomenta el espíritu escolar, sino que utiliza su **entusiasmo** y energía para unir al equipo y al público.

**FUN FACT** — **DATO CURIOSO**

The record for the largest team cheer was 2,102 cheerleaders in Hangzhou, Zhejiang, China. It featured people who were as young as 5 years old and as old as 68. The event was big enough to end up in the Guinness Book of World Records!

El récord para el mayor equipo de porrismo fue de 2 102 porristas en Hangzhou, Zhejiang, China. En él participaron personas desde cinco años hasta los 68. ¡El evento fue lo suficientemente grande como para terminar en El libro Guinness de los récords!

A good cheerleading squad uses music, dance, and athleticism to **energize** and entertain the crowd. Some would argue that they get as much exercise as the players they cheer for!

Un buen equipo de porristas o animadoras utiliza la música, el baile y el atletismo para **energizar** y entretener al público. Algunos dirán que hacen tanto ejercicio como los jugadores a los que animan.

# TRYOUTS
# PRUEBAS

Like many high school sports, cheerleaders compete to make the team. Every high school is different, but for many the **tryout** process lasts an entire week. Participants will learn a cheer and dance each day.

Al igual que en muchos deportes de secundaria, las porristas compiten para entrar a un equipo. Cada escuela es diferente, pero para muchas el proceso de **pruebas** dura una semana entera. Las participantes aprenderán una animación y un baile cada día.

On the day of tryouts, there are usually three to five judges who will score on categories such as spirit, ability, and eye contact.

El día de las pruebas, suele haber entre tres y cinco jueces que califican categorías como el esfuerzo, la habilidad y el contacto visual.

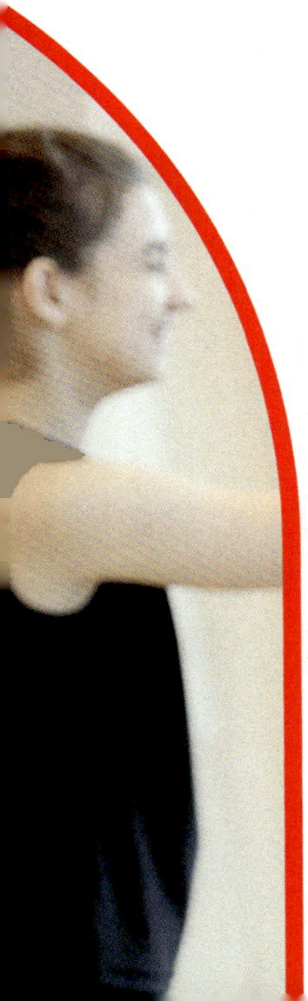

**FUN FACT** **DATO CURIOSO**

There are around 3.5 million cheerleaders in the United States alone.

Hay alrededor de 3.5 millones de animadoras solo en Estados Unidos.

# VARSITY AND JUNIOR VARSITY TEAMS

# EQUIPOS UNIVERSITARIOS Y UNIVERSITARIOS *JUNIOR*

High school cheerleading squads are often divided by sport and by classes. The JV (Junior Varsity) squads are usually made up of first- and second-year students. This squad is where cheerleaders will learn the basics while cheering for JV teams.

Junior Varsity
Universitario *junior*

Los equipos de porristas de las escuelas secundarias suelen estar divididos por deportes y por clases. Los equipos universitarios *junior* (JV, por sus siglas en inglés) suelen estar formados por estudiantes de primer y segundo año. En este equipo, las porristas aprenden lo básico mientras animan a los equipos JV.

The varsity level squads are mostly third- or fourth-year cheerleaders. Varsity cheerleaders can often do more advanced dance moves and **gymnastics** as they cheer for the varsity level teams.

Las escuadras de nivel universitario están formadas en su mayoría por animadoras de tercer o cuarto año. Las porristas de nivel universitario a menudo pueden hacer movimientos de baile y **gimnasia** más avanzados mientras animan a los equipos de nivel universitario.

Varsity
Universitario

Cheerleaders were historically seen at high school football or basketball games, but that has changed over the years. Some cheerleading squads make appearances at baseball, soccer, volleyball, and wrestling matches. Every sports crowd could use some help cheering!

Históricamente, las porristas se veían en los partidos de fútbol americano o baloncesto de las escuelas secundarias, pero eso ha cambiado con los años. Algunas escuadras de animadoras hacen apariciones en partidos de béisbol, fútbol, voleibol y lucha libre. ¡Todos los espectadores deportivos podrían animar a sus equipos!

# ROLES IN CHEERLEADING
# ROLES EN EL PORRISMO

There are three basic roles in most cheerleading squads. They are:

**Flyer** — The cheerleader lifted up or tossed into the air is a flyer. They end up as the center of attention. It might look easy, but a flyer's role is physically **demanding**... and dangerous.

**Bases** — The foundation of any stunt that launches or lifts the flyer into the air is a base. They are usually taller and stronger and use good technique to keep themselves and flyers from getting hurt.

**Spotter** — Similar to a base, spotters are used to help steady or balance cheerleading stunts. They are also the first point of contact when a flyer **dismounts** or falls.

Hay tres funciones básicas en la mayoría de los equipos de porristas. Estas son:

**Voladora:** La porrista levantada o lanzada al aire es una voladora. Acaba siendo el centro de atención. Puede parecer fácil, pero el papel de una voladora es físicamente **exigente**... y peligroso.

**Base:** El soporte de cualquier acrobacia que lance o eleve en el aire a la voladora es una base. Suelen ser más altas y fuertes, y utilizan una buena técnica para evitar que tanto ellas como las voladoras se hagan daño.

**Cuidadora:** Al igual que la base, las cuidadoras se utilizan para ayudar a estabilizar o equilibrar las acrobacias de las porristas. También son el primer punto de contacto cuando una voladora se **desmonta** o se cae.

FLYER
VOLADORA

SPOTTER
CUIDADORA

BASE
BASE

# EQUIPMENT & UNIFORMS
# EQUIPAMIENTO Y UNIFORMES

Cheerleaders will often use pom-poms, usually in the school's colors, to attract attention. Many use megaphones to boost the volume of their voice.

Las porristas suelen utilizar pompones, normalmente con los colores de la escuela, para llamar la atención. Muchas utilizan megáfonos para aumentar el volumen de su voz.

Megaphone
Megáfono

Most cheerleading squads wear uniforms displaying their school colors and mascot. Girls typically wear skirts and boys usually wear athletic pants. Both wear similar sleeveless shirts. In colder weather, warmer pants and sweaters are worn.

La mayoría de los equipos de animadoras lleva uniformes con los colores de la escuela y la mascota. Las chicas suelen llevar falda y los chicos suelen llevar pantalones deportivos. Ambos llevan camisetas sin mangas similares. Cuando hace más frío, usan pantalones y suéteres más abrigados.

**FUN FACT** — **DATO CURIOSO**

The word pom-pom comes from the French word *pompe*, which means tuft of ribbons.

La palabra pompón proviene de la palabra francesa *pompe*, que significa mechón o listones.

# CHEERS, CHANTING, AND PEP RALLIES

# ANIMACIONES, CANTOS Y CONCENTRACIONES PARA ANIMAR

One of the biggest goals for a cheerleading squad is to boost the crowd's energy. Many cheers and chants are about team pride and school spirit.

Uno de los principales objetivos de un equipo de porristas es aumentar la energía del público. Muchos de los gritos y cantos tienen que ver con el orgullo del equipo y el espíritu escolar.

Some high schools hold pep rallies. These are school gatherings to generate excitement before a big game. Often cheerleaders will lead these rallies to cheer and perform dance routines. The school band will play music to get the crowd going.

Algunas escuelas celebran concentraciones para animar. Se trata de reuniones escolares para generar entusiasmo antes de un gran partido. A menudo, las porristas dirigen estas concentraciones para animar y realizar rutinas de baile. La banda de música de la escuela toca para animar a la multitud.

# DANCING AND STUNTING
# BAILES Y ACROBACIAS

Most times, cheerleading is about entertaining the spectators at the game. To do this, some cheerleading squads play music and perform a dance routine to pump up the crowd.

La mayoría de las veces, las porristas se dedican a entretener a los espectadores del partido. Para ello, algunos equipos de porristas tocan música y realizan una rutina de baile para animar al público.

Some more advanced cheerleading teams might perform what is called stunting. This can include lifting cheerleaders into the air, doing gymnastics, or forming a human **pyramid** with the entire crew.

Algunos equipos de porristas más avanzados pueden realizar lo que se denomina acrobacias. Esto puede incluir levantar a las porristas en el aire, hacer gimnasia o formar una **pirámide** humana con todo el equipo.

**FUN FACT — DATO CURIOSO**

In 2017, the largest cheer pyramid was made up of 60 girls in New Zealand. The feat landed them in the Guinness Book of World Records.

En 2017, la mayor pirámide de animación estaba formada por 60 chicas en Nueva Zelanda. La hazaña les hizo entrar a El libro Guinness de los récords.

# PRACTICE AND CHEERLEADING CAMPS

# PRÁCTICAS Y CAMPAMENTOS DE PORRISMO

Like any high-impact sport, cheerleading takes lots of practice. Most squads will practice stunting and dances after school. They want to make sure they're ready to perform in front of the crowd.

Como en cualquier deporte de alto impacto, las porristas necesitan mucha práctica. La mayoría de los equipos practica acrobacias y bailes después de la escuela. Quieren asegurarse de estar preparadas para actuar ante el público.

Many places offer cheerleading camps where cheerleaders can stay to improve their skills. Campers will form closer team bonds and work on **tumbling**, dance moves, and team stunts.

Muchos lugares ofrecen campamentos para porristas, donde pueden alojarse para mejorar sus habilidades. En los campamentos se estrechan los lazos de equipo, se trabajan las **volteretas**, los movimientos de baile y las acrobacias en equipo.

**The National Cheerleading Association (NCA) was founded in 1948 by former cheerleader Lawrence Herkimer. He believed cheerleaders could perform better if they trained outside the school year. He started the first cheer training camp the very next year in 1949.**

**La Asociación Nacional de Porrismo (NCA, por sus siglas en inglés), fue fundada en 1948 por el exporrista Lawrence Herkimer. Él creía que las porristas podían rendir más si se entrenaban fuera del curso escolar. Al año siguiente, en 1949, puso en marcha el primer campamento de porrismo.**

# FRIDAY NIGHT GAMES
# JUEGOS DE VIERNES POR LA NOCHE

Cheerleaders are an important part of high school football games. Most schools have their games on Friday night under the bright lights on a crisp, autumn evening.

Las porristas son una parte importante de los partidos de fútbol de las escuelas secundarias. La mayoría de las escuelas celebra sus partidos los viernes por la noche bajo las brillantes luces de una fresca tarde de otoño.

During these popular games, cheerleaders often tailor their cheers to what's happening in the game. The noise from the stands and the sidelines reminds the players on the field that everyone is counting on them to bring home the win!

Durante estos partidos populares, las porristas suelen adaptar sus cantos a lo que ocurre en el juego. ¡El ruido de las gradas y de las bandas les recuerda a los jugadores que están en el campo de juego que todos cuentan con que ellos ganen!

# CHEERLEADING COMPETITIONS
# COMPETENCIAS DE PORRISMO

The athletes cheerleaders support aren't the only ones who get to compete! Cheerleading has become such a **competitive** sport that there's a national championship held every year.

Los atletas a los que apoyan las porristas no son los únicos que compiten. El porrismo se ha convertido en un deporte tan **competitivo** que cada año se celebra un campeonato nacional.

**FUN FACT** **DATO CURIOSO**

The most recent NHSCC competition featured 950 teams! Squads from 34 states in the United States and 9 countries competed in the 2020 competition.

En la última competencia de la NHSCC participaron 950 equipos. Escuadras de 34 estados de Estados Unidos y de nueve países compitieron en el campeonato de 2020.

The National High School Cheerleading Championship (NHSCC) happens annually in Orlando, Florida. The best high school cheerleading squads from around the country and world compete to see who is number one!

El Campeonato Nacional de Porristas de Secundaria (NHSCC, por sus siglas en inglés) se celebra anualmente en Orlando, Florida. ¡Los mejores equipos de porristas de escuelas secundarias de todo el país y del mundo compiten para ver quién es el número uno!

# CONCLUSION
# CONCLUSIÓN

Cheerleading is one of the most action-packed sports high-schoolers participate in. It takes skill, energy, and school spirit to come out on top. Games really wouldn't be the same without cheerleaders.

El porrismo es uno de los deportes con más acción en los que participan los estudiantes de secundaria. Se necesita habilidad, energía y espíritu escolar para llegar a la cima. Los partidos no serían lo mismo sin las porristas.

Will you practice your backflips and perform in front of the crowd? Maybe you and your squad will go to the nationals. With practice and dedication, you'll see why cheerleading is definitely one of the TOP HIGH SCHOOL SPORTS!

¿Practicarás tus saltos hacia atrás y actuarás ante el público? Tal vez tú y tu equipo vayan a los campeonatos nacionales. Con práctica y dedicación, verás por qué el porrismo es definitivamente uno de los ¡MEJORES DEPORTES DE LA ESCUELA SECUNDARIA!

# GLOSSARY

**ACL** (AY-SEE-EL): an abbreviation for anterior cruciate ligament, a body part that stabilizes the knee joint

**competitive** (kuhm-PET-uh-tiv): attempting to be as good or better than others

**demanding** (di-MAN-ding): a task requiring skill and effort

**dismounts** (diss-MOUNTS): finishing moves of students or gymnastics tricks

**energize** (EN-ur-jize): to supply energy to something

**enthusiasm** (en-THOO-zee-az-uhm): intense excitement

**gymnastics** (jim-NASS-tiks): a sport that displays physical agility and coordination

**pyramid** (PIHR-uh-mid): a triangular shape with a large base and a pointy top

**spectators** (SPEK-tay-turz): people in a crowd gathered to watch

**tryout** (TRY-out): to test the potential of a person or thing

**tumbling** (TUM-bul-ing): performing acrobatic or gymnastic exercises

# GLOSARIO

**competitivo:** Que intenta ser tan bueno o mejor que los demás.

**desmonta:** Cuando se terminan los movimientos de los estudiantes o las piruetas de gimnasia.

**energizar:** Suministrar energía a alguien o a algo.

**entusiasmo:** Emoción intensa.

**espectadores:** Personas que se reúnen en una multitud para observar.

**exigente:** Tarea que requiere habilidad y esfuerzo.

**gimnasia:** Deporte que requiere agilidad y coordinación física.

**LCA:** Abreviatura de ligamento cruzado anterior, una parte del cuerpo que estabiliza la articulación de la rodilla.

**pirámide:** Forma triangular con una base grande y una parte superior puntiaguda.

**pruebas:** Ensayos para ver el potencial de una persona o cosa.

**volteretas:** Ejercicios acrobáticos o gimnásticos.

# INDEX



# ÍNDICE ANALÍTICO



# WEBSITES TO VISIT
# SITIOS WEB PARA VISITAR

https://kids.kiddle.co/Cheerleader

https://kids.britannica.com/students/article/cheerleading/319406

# ABOUT THE AUTHOR

Thomas Kingsley Troupe is the author of a big ol' pile of books for kids. He's written about everything from ghosts to Bigfoot to third grade werewolves. He even wrote a book about dirt. When he's not writing or reading, he gets plenty of exercise and remembers sacking quarterbacks while on his high school football team. Thomas lives in Woodbury, Minnesota with his two sons.

# SOBRE EL AUTOR

Thomas Kingsley Troupe es el autor de muchísimos libros para niños. Ha escrito sobre todo tipo de temas, desde fantasmas hasta de Pie Grande, y de hombres lobo de tercer grado. Escribió incluso un libro sobre la suciedad. Cuando no está escribiendo o leyendo, hace mucho ejercicio y se acuerda de cómo derribaba mariscales de campo contrarios cuando estaba en el equipo de fútbol de la escuela secundaria. Thomas vive en Woodbury, Minnesota, con sus dos hijos.


**Crabtree Publishing**

**crabtreebooks.com 800-387-7650**





Written by/Escrito por: Thomas Kingsley Troupe
Designer/Diseñadora: Jennifer Dydyk
Editor/Editora: Kelli Hicks
Proofreader/Correctora de pruebas: Ellen Rodger
Translated by/Traducción de: Santiago Ochoa
Spanish-language layout and proofread/
Maquetación y corrección en español: Base Tres
Production manager/Coordinadora de producción:
Candice Campbell

Hardcover 978-1-0398-6932-5
Paperback 978-1-0398-6911-0
Ebook (pdf) 978-1-0398-6953-0
Epub 978-1-0398-6974-5

**Published in Canada**
**Publicado en Canadá**
**Crabtree Publishing**
616 Welland Avenue
St. Catharines, Ontario
L2M 5V6

**Published in the United States**
**Publicado en los Estados Unidos**
**Crabtree Publishing**
347 Fifth Avenue
Suite 1402-145
New York, NY 10016

Photographs: Cover background pattern (and pattern throughout book © HNK/Shutterstock.com, pom pom on cover and title page © Dana Zurkiyeh/Shutterstock.com, cover photo of cheerleaders © Thomas Carter | Dreamstime.com. Following images from Shutterstock.com: Page 4 top photo © Rob Byron, bottom photo © Poznyakov, Page 5 © View Apart, Page 6 © chippix, Page 9 top photo © nullplus, bottom photo © Aleksei Lazukov, Page 10 © Pressmaster, Page 12 bottom photo © Joseph Sohm, Page 13 and Page 15 (spotter) © WoodysPhotos, Page 15 (base) © Cherednychenko Ihor, Page 16 bottom photo © WoodysPhotos, Page 17 © LightField Studios, Page 18 © Joseph Sohm, Page 19 bottom photo © JoeSAPhotos, Page 23 top photo © Richard Thornton, bottom photo © TommyStockProject, Page 25 top photo © Joseph Sohm, Page 27 bottom photo © Pavel L Photo and Video, Page 29 bottom photo © nullplus. Following images from istock by Getty Images: Pages 8, 11, top photo Page 19, bottom photo Page 25, top photos Pages 27 and 29 © Roberto Galan, Page 12 top photo © Joseph Calomeni, Page 22 © marieclaudelemay, Following images from Dreamstime.com: Page 15 (flyer) Pavel Losevsky, Page 16 top photo © Sports Images, Page 19 top photo © Molly Williams, Page 20 © Aspenphoto, Page 21 top photo © Joe Sohm, bottom photo Thomas Carter, Page 24 © Joe Sohm, Page 26 © Ritmoboxer, Page 28 © Reinout Van Wagtendonk. Page 7 photo courtesy of the Library of Congress

Printed in the U.S.A./Impreso en los Estados Unidos/CP112025

**Library and Archives Canada Cataloguing in Publication**
Available at the Library and Archives Canada

**Library of Congress Cataloging-in-Publication Data**
Available at the Library of Congress